YODA

THE DARING, DAUNTLESS, DARLING CAT

Written & Illustrated

by

Joan A. de Bruin

Cover design by Chloe Annetts
www.chloeartanddesign.com

Published by Mediacs
www.mediacs.com

ISBN: 978-0-9673134-3-6

This book is dedicated to Doctor Victoria Ibric and her husband, Doctor Andrew Peterson, who live with our darling Yoda, putting up with all her shenanigans. And, to Doctor Victoria, who encouraged me and shared Yoda's unbelievable real life stories with me.

AND

To Amelia Ward, who saved Yoda's life when she was three weeks old, and to Tiger aka Maxwell her beloved cat. Nor can I forget the Neurofeedback clients, Doctors and friends of Doctor Victoria who fed and loved Yoda when she was tiny. I can't leave out Easy, the dog, Yoda's best buddy.

AND

To Chuck Davis, inventor of the ROSHI system. To Elizabeth Julia Stoumen, who sensitively edited and proofread the script. To Jim Bergman, Mediacs.com, who brought our dream to fruition, a published book. And, to my friends and colleagues who suffered through Yoda's early drafts.

AND

To the Neurofeedback & NeuroRehab Institute, Inc., Doctor Victoria Ibric, President, who engaged me to write the story of Yoda and to illustrate her journey. And, for her photographic talent which provided the photos used within the collaged, inked and painted illustrations.

Table of Contents

Chapter One

When I was a tiny baby kitten, a big girl named Amelia found me. I was sitting in the middle of a road. Huge cars and trucks rushed by. Big black tires squealed. Horns honked. A big wind pushed me around. My fur stood on end. I was so scared I hid my head between my paws. I cried, "Mommy! Mom...my! Where are you?"

Amelia Saving Baby Yoda

Amelia carried me to her big yellow car. She said, "Oh my, what big blue eyes you have. Why would anyone leave a pretty girl like you all alone?"

The car stopped in front of a giant building. Amelia put me in a straw basket and carried me inside. "Stop," I mewed, "where are you taking me? Where's my mommy? I'm hungry!" I meowed as loud as I could.

"It's okay little girl. You're safe with me." Amelia fluffed my fur. "Oh my, what soft fur you have."

Bump! I rolled against the side of the basket. "Ow," I mewed. On that note I opened my eyes really wide. I saw giant faces staring down at me. They were huge and scary. I shut my eyes real tight so no one could see me.

Suddenly, I was lifted out of the basket. I struggled every which way, my feet wiggling in the air. I hissed and spit at my new Mommy, who I didn't know was my new Human Mommy until later.

"Little girl," she said, "I love you already. You don't have to be afraid." Human Mommy's voice sounded like gentle falling rain. My heart melted.

Human Mommy picked me up. I laid my furry face against her smooth face. Her skin was like silk. I sniffed her cheek. She smelled like sweet milk. I patted the top of her head with my paw. It was covered with soft fluffy hair, sort of like fur. I purred and purred, rubbing my head against her face. I sighed. "You're my mommy now for ever and ever."

A moment later she put me back in the basket. This time on a soft fuzzy blanket. I cried, "No, no, Human Mommy! I want to stay with you." I scrunched up my face and howled. "Don't leave me. I'm hungry!"

"I'll be right back baby face. I know exactly what you need." Human Mommy's mouth stretched in a great big smile.

I thought Human Mommy might disappear like my Fur Mommy. I desperately looked from side to side, trying to find her. I chirrup-meowed, calling her to me. "Where are you?" I cried.

In the blink of an eye Human Mommy was back. She looked down at me, smiling. "Tsk, tsk, my little scaredy cat. You're safe." She lifted me out of the basket, untangling me from the blanket. In her hand she was holding a "my size" bottle. I could smell the baby kitty milk. She pushed the nipple into my mouth. I tasted the warm, sweet milk. I sucked and sucked until my tummy nearly burst.

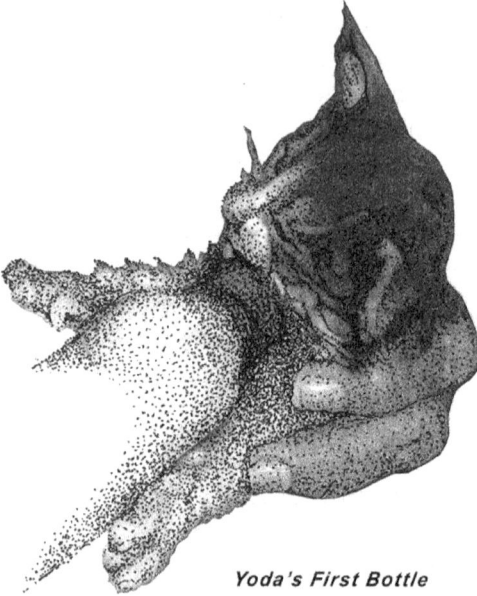

Yoda's First Bottle

Warm and full, I curled up in my blanket and dreamt about Fur Mommy and my Fur Brothers and Sisters. We were happily suckling on Fur Mommy's breasts. Then we fell asleep, purring, cuddling and curling on her belly. She smelled like home.

"Oh baby kitty," Human Mommy laughed gently. "The milk is running down your chin. Look here, you've grown a milk mustache. Got it," she said, wiping my face with a napkin.

I shook my head. It tickled.

Human Mommy took me to her home in Amelia's basket. I slept there every night. Then in the daytime she'd take me to her job. The big faces weren't scary anymore. They admired me and petted me and fed me. Everyone wanted me, but I still missed my Fur Mommy.

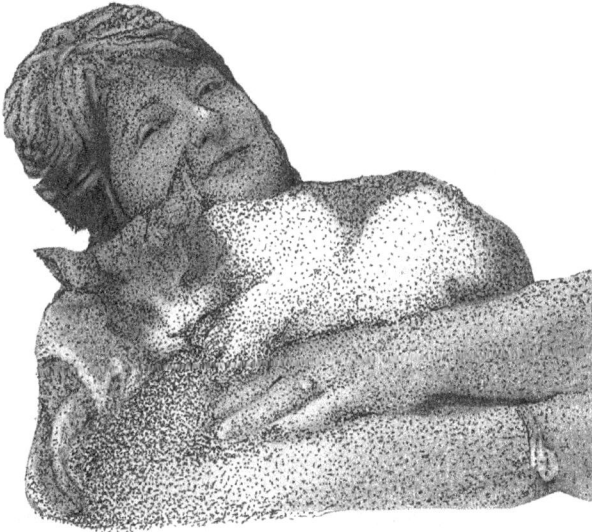

Human Mommy Cuddling Yoda

In the nighttime, I'd wake up every two hours and cry for milk. Human Mommy would come running with my bottle. She never left me alone when I called her, not once. She'd cuddle me like my Fur Mommy, kiss me, and tell me how much she loved me. I would purr and purr and purr. I was in kitten heaven. I had a home.

YODA

Chapter Two

One night, Human Mommy said, "Little girl, we've got to find a name for you. Maybe your new Papa has an idea? Papa," she called, "come here."

Human Papa looked me over with his all seeing eye. "Mommy, have you ever seen huge furry ears on such a wee kitten? Her face looks like Yoda in the Star Wars movie. What do you think?"

"Perfect!" Human Mommy exclaimed. "Yoda she is."

Human Papa put me on his shoulder. I rubbed my face against his face. His beard was scratchy, not soft like fur, but I loved him anyway. Every night, I would jump on his round belly and settle down for a nap. He'd stroke my head until I fell asleep.

I'm grew taller, bigger and longer every day. My fur grew extra soft and thick. My tail grew without end, long and bushy. One day, on its own, my tail knocked over a glass of water. I got wet and yowled to high heavens. Cats hate water.

I didn't understand what happened to me. I was different from who I was as a kitten. I didn't know myself anymore. I had turned into a roaring train on four feet, running amuck, not listening when I was told to stop running around like a batty bat. I was one mixed up cat.

Easy is a grownup dog who lives with us. He has thick black fur and a fat tummy. Even though he was getting old and stiff, he still wanted to play. I'd lie on my back and bat his snout with my paws. He'd woof at me to stop but I didn't. What makes me mad is that every morning Human Papa takes Easy for walks in front of our condo, and I have to stay home.

Human Mommy said I had become a drama queen. If I were a human girl, I'd have run into my room, cry, and slam the door. I'm a cat so I don't slam doors, but I did blow everything out of proportion. There was the time Easy stepped on my tail. I yelled so loud our next door neighbor came over to ask what was wrong.

Human Mommy bought cat treats for me. We played the jump game. She held up a treat. I jumped in the air and grab it with my teeth. Because I'm big now, I drink water out of a bowl, eat grownup cat food, and don't drink milk from a kitty bottle.

One time I was so mad at Easy, I tried to roar like a lion. He'd eaten my cat treat, again! I opened my mouth wide, all set to let loose a mighty roar, but not even a tiny mew came out. You can imagine my embarrassment.

Human Papa's laugher filled the room. "Did you see that Mommy? Yoda tried to roar. She thinks she's a big bad cat from Africa. Sorry Yoda, I'm only teasing. I love you even if you can't roar. I hid under the couch for the rest of the day.

One morning I woke up before anyone else. I ran downstairs and saw this funny tree. It hadn't been there when I went to bed the night before. I stretched my neck to see to the top. Mini-lights blinked off and on, twinkling and winking. There were red balls and green balls and yellow balls. An angel spread her wings at the very top. She was pretty with a gold dress and a crown.

"Oh boy," I mewed. I lifted my paw and batted at one of the balls. Bang! The red ball flew high in the air, bounced against the wall, hit the floor and broke into a million pieces. My eyes opened wide. "Wow!" I cried. Bang, crash! Bang, crash! Bang, crash! There were smashed balls everywhere.

I was in the midst of my fun when Human Mommy ran down the stairs and grabbed me. I squirmed in her arms and accidentally scratched her.

"Ow! Stop, Yoda! Stop it right now! You're ruining our holiday tree. Listen to me! Stop right this instant!"

Naughty Yoda in the Holiday Tree

I didn't stop. I jumped out of her arms and quick as a flash jumped back into the tree. I dove from branch to branch, batting more balls to the ground. I climbed higher and higher and higher. I looked down. My eyes narrowed. I put my ears back and hissed at Human Mommy.

"I'm a big cat now. What are you going to do about it?" I knocked down the angel from her high perch. She landed on her head and broke.

You think that was all I did? Not a chance. I loved to jump high on the wall in the front room. I was like a Mexican jumping bean. Bing! Bang! Boom! I'd hit the wall and land, bam, on the floor. Then I'd be off again, up and running like a spider along the wall. Then, I'd land again, bam, on the floor. I'd play my wall game day in and day out. Human Mommy and Papa would tell me to stop, but I couldn't. The only time I was quiet was when I was asleep.

Once in a while I'd get angry and nip Human Mommy's cheek. I'd arch my back and puff up my fur to make me look bigger than life. I'd dance around the room on my tiptoes, trying to look mean. Then, for real, she'd know how mad I was at her. I didn't dare puff up at Papa.

"Eating Human Mommy's plants was fun too. The leaves would bounce and bounce when I hit them. The plants couldn't get away. They were stuck in their planters and had no feet, only roots. I was told, "NO!" That word didn't stop me. I'd chew on and on, even the nasty tasting plants.

Human Papa got upset with me too. I run up and down the stairs all day, at least a hundred times. I'd stick my whole body into the fireplace.

Then I'd make black footprints all over the house. Papa would chase after me, cleaning the floor behind me. He'd grumble like Grumpy in Snow White, calling me bad Yoda. But I'm not bad. I'm good.

Human Papa Scolding Yoda

I was sorry a lot for what I did, but I couldn't help myself. Why couldn't I obey my Human Mommy and Papa? I love them and Easy. I thought something was wrong with me. I'd lose interest in one game and have to run to another. Even when I was dreaming, I'd be running somewhere or looking for something I couldn't find... I mewed sadly in my sleep.

Chapter Three

A Contrary Yoda Eating Mommy's Plant

Early one morning, Human Mommy sat me down on a chair. She looked me straight in the eye. "Yoda," she said, "this behavior has to stop. Quit squirming. Settle down this minute! This is serious. You can't seem to focus on any one thing for more than a second. One moment you're climbing the wall. Next you're eating my plants and breaking ornaments on our holiday tree. Now you're fighting with Easy, who's your friend. I caught you the other day biting his snout."

"You don't understand. I'm not like other cats." I scratched my ear, mewing softly, sadly.

"I try to tell you but you don't understand. I can't stop myself. My brain is all catty-wonka. My mind tells me to jump and play as fast as I can, even when I don't want to. "

I used every gesture and sound in CAT language to help Human Mommy understand my confusion, but it was no use. I meowed in a large voice. "Can't you hear me?"

Human Mommy only looked more confused than ever.

I looked this way and that, spied my favorite mouse toy, jumped out of the chair and slid under the couch to retrieve it. "Oh, that's where I left that stupid mouse. I forgot. I'm always forgetting."

"Yoda! Come out from under that couch. Your doctor told me you'd grow out of this nonsense but you haven't. You're hurting me with your biting and scratching. Look at the scratches on my arm. You can't focus on anything for more than a second. And all your crazy running around. Something's not right. We need to see what's going on."

Yoda Flying Over Easy the Dog

"Can't you stop yelling at me," I meowed. The mouse dropped out of my mouth. I scooted back out from under the couch and headed for the sliding glass doors. I stared through the window at the birds chattering in the tree.

"Oh boy, I wonder what one would taste like? Hmmm, I bet they'd taste all fluttery and crunchy in my mouth." I licked my chops. Human Mommy says birds aren't for my eating. What a silly thing to say. They eat chicken don't they? It's a bird, isn't it? So why can't I eat a bird?

"Yoda, I've made an appointment for you with Doctor Ligya. She loves cats and will know just what to do."

What did she say? My ears pricked up. I forgot the birds. I turned around to face Human Mommy. "There's nothing wrong with me," I said. "I'll be a good girl. I promise. Please don't send me away."

"Yoda," Human Papa crooned, picking me up in his arms. "The Doctor will help you feel better." He patted me on the head. "Don't you worry, my pretty Yoda. We love you."

Chapter Four

Yoda Meets the Cat Whisperer,
Dr. Ligya, Maxwell, and Blueberry

Human Mommy drove me in her car. I lay next
to her on the seat listening to a beautiful violin
playing on the radio. This was only the second
time I've ridden in a car, and I love it. Just being
out of the condo was a relief. I'm unique among

cats, so I'm told. Before long, we stopped under a shady tree in front of an old Victorian House.

The house had a wide porch lined with rocking chairs. Cats of all colors sat on the rockers, shining themselves in the sun, preening and chatting with their friends. They didn't look up as Human Mommy carried me up the steps. There was a small plaque above the door. "See that Yoda? We've arrived at The Cat Hill Brain Training Academy."

There was an arrow, directing visitors to the parlor. The room was empty except for us. We sat down. A door opened and I heard. "Oh, so this is Yoda. I'm Doctor Ligya." She smiled warmly at me and Human Mommy. "Please come into my office. Can I offer either of you a glass or a bowl of water?"

"No thank you, not for me," Human Mommy said, "but Yoda is probably thirsty."

"Good morning Yoda," Doctor Ligya said. "Jump up on my desk so I can see you. We have lots to discuss." She poured water into a small bowl. "Here you are girl."

I took a flying leap out of Human Mommy's arms and landed smack dab in front of the Doctor. "Oh my," I mewed. I sat up as straight as an arrow. My eyes got big. My mouth opened wide. I could have swallowed a fish whole.

"She's not speaking human. She's speaking CAT."

"Yes, I certainly did." Doctor Ligya smiled, her eyes sparkled. Then she turned to Human Mommy. "When I was a child, I learned to speak CAT. I know it must look odd to you because I have to use a special sign language along with gesture and voice. It's a very physical language. Quite beautiful really, like ballet and opera rolled into one. I'll translate for you as we move along."

I couldn't take my eyes off of Doctor Ligya. She had blue eyes like mine and black, black hair. Her face and body resembled my Human Mama. Her hands never stopped moving when she talked. Maybe she'd like to be my fairy Godmother? She sure looked like one.

"Don't be concerned, Yoda's Mommy." Doctor Ligya said, "You've heard of the Dog Whisperer? Yes, I see you have. I'm a Cat Whisperer. I help cats and their human companions to resolve problems with my gift. Yoda will be playing a special game on a computer to help her heal her brain. It's called Neurofeedback."

Wow, I thought, it sounds like Human Papa's computer game when he lets me chase the arrow around on the screen with my paw. I haven't caught the arrow yet but someday I will.

I purred and purred, daydreaming, thinking about that day.

"Okay, Yoda. It's your turn. Tell me what's been going on." Doctor Ligya lightly scratched my head.

I snapped out of my daydream and talked and talked. I told Doctor Ligya all about me. How my Fur Mommy left me. How I missed my brothers and sisters. How I was scared my Human Mommy and Papa would leave me. How I talked all the time, even to the plants, but didn't listen to anybody. How I got stung by a bee when I climbed up the screen door. How I wasn't interested in anything, but everything. How I've never had a cat friend. I yowled aloud my unhappiness and disappointment in myself.

"I understand, Yoda." Doctor Ligya listened to my every word. Her eyes were warm with compassion. "Don't you worry, Yoda. I'll explain everything to your Human Mommy. We're going to have you visit us twice a week until you're better. Would you like that?"

"Me...ow," I answered. "Thank you."

I jumped back into Human Mommy's arms. This was the longest conversation I'd ever had without running off to do something else. Pretty amazing, I thought. My eyes were drawn to the huge window behind Doctor Ligya. I saw cats and more cats, playing and laughing. I sighed with longing. I wanted to be with them.

Doctor Ligya looked across the desk at my Human Mommy. "We will help Yoda change the way she lives in the world. Her mind is playing tricks on her and she needs to regain focus. Her brain will be learning and creating new pathways to follow. She'll become more aware of what's happening around her and be able to respond, rather than react.

"Regarding Yoda's abandonment issues – not too surprising knowing she was left in the street when she was three weeks old. We'll be assisting her with those fears as well."

The Doctor stood up, holding out her hand. "Yoda wants to change. That's the first big step. I saw her looking wistfully at the cats playing in the yard. They've all had Brain Training or Neurofeedback. Yoda was seeing the happy results. We'll see you both in a couple days."

Chapter Five

Human Mommy and I were sitting and talking with Doctor Ligya when we heard a deep baritone meow at the door, followed by a clawing sound. The door swung open.

"Maxwell. Thanks for dropping by." Doctor Ligya waved him to the top of her desk. "Yoda, come sit beside Maxwell."

I landed lightly next to the muscle-bound tabby cat. He turned his head and looked down at me. Boy, I thought, is he ever big and tough looking. He had one ear missing, a scar running down the side of his nose and a stubby tail. His short, rough fur was black with brown and yellow patches. He was big scary, like he could bite off my face.

"I'd like to introduce Maxwell," Doctor Ligya said, gesturing in CAT. He's one of our greatest successes. He teaches cat lore to our young ones. It's important they know who they are and where they come from."

I sat silently, not moving a muscle. I couldn't move.

Doctor Ligya looked around the two cats at Yoda's Mommy. "I'll be translating CAT to human. You'll be able to understand our conversation that way. "She took out a notebook and pen from her desk. "Maxwell, thanks for being here to share your story with Yoda and her Human Mommy."

I stretched out on the cool desk top and waited. Then Maxwell narrowed his eyes and wiggled his stump of a tail.

"Okay, Maxwell," she grinned, "don't get your tail in a wad. I'll tell them. Just today, Maxwell told me that Amelia saved Yoda's life and then recommended you bring Yoda to us."

"Yoda?" Maxwell said, sniffing my nose, "When I came to Doctor Ligya, I was a mess. Amelia found me at this place called an animal shelter. Even though I was a grownup cat, she picked me with my ugly face and all its scars, and my broken tail. She saw something special in me and took me home.

"At first, I tried to bite and scratch her. I was afraid she'd hurt me. I'd pee on the floor and do other bad things. I had been living on the street since I was a kitten, eating out of garbage cans and fighting other cats over a scrap of food. I had no home. No family.

"When Amelia brought me to Doctor Ligya, I spit and hissed and yowled to keep her away. I tried to run, but her door was closed. I threw myself against the door until I was exhausted.

"Once I calmed down, Doctor Ligya asked me if I wanted to change. I thought and thought as I lay hurting on the floor. I knew I didn't want to end up in a dark smelly alley again with only rotten food to eat. I wanted a home.

"Somehow, the Doctor's message hit me right where I lived. I wouldn't be the cat you see today if I'd said, no. I don't run around like I used to. I'm everybody's big brother, being the old guy I am. I help the young'uns with their problems and I'm happy, not scared like I was before."

"Thank you, Maxwell." Doctor Ligya said. "You'd better rejoin your friends. I see them staring up at my window." She laughed. "There's Blueberry mewing for you on the window sill."

"See ya' later, girly-girl!" Bam! Maxwell hit the floor and was gone.

My head was spinning like a top. The room was dead silent with Maxwell was gone. I watched him through the window frolicking like a kitten with Blueberry and his other friends. Oh, if only I could be with Maxwell and his friends.

"I'd like to begin Yoda on mind-training right away," Human Mommy said. "Your interpretation of CAT language was incredible. I had no idea she was suffering that much. I used to yell at her. I didn't know. Hearing Yoda and Maxwell through you convinced me. Can you tell Yoda how sorry I am?"

"She already knows. She loves you and her papa very much.

Chapter Six

We arrived right on time for my first appointment. Maxwell waved his paw at me from a distance and I waved back. Blueberry smiled at me.

Doctor Ligya took me into a small room with a cat-shaped chair. A computer sat on the table in front of me. Human Mommy sat behind me.

"How are you today, my Yoda?" Doctor Ligya asked. "Are you ready for your first lesson?"

"I think so," I whispered, "but I'm a little scared."

"New experiences make us scared sometimes," Dr. Ligya smiled in her gentle way, "but it won't be long before the strangeness goes away. I promise."

I smiled up at her and jumped into the cat chair.

"Yoda. Now I'm placing these special clips, like earrings, to your ears. Don't move, honey. They won't hurt you. Next, we're going to fasten colored dots on different places on your head. The dots have wires coming from them. These are fastened to the computer so your mind can play fun games."

I squirmed and squirmed. I could hardly stay still in one place.

"Try to relax, sweet girl," Doctor Ligya placed her hand on my back. "I'm going to start the game. You're going to help Sir Puss-in-Boots catch the mouse. Puss is chasing the mouse through a rocky maze of tunnels. When Puss catches the mouse, game's over." She winked at me. "Now, here's the fun part. You're going to make Puss chase the mouse with your mind. Don't," she warned, "try to grab the mouse with your paws. It won't work. Do you think you'd like to try?"

"Right on, Doc!" I cried in CAT, wiggling in excitement. "We're a go!"

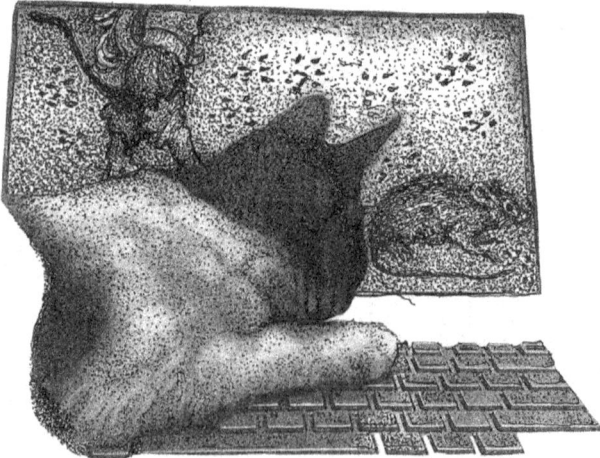

Yoda Playing the Puss-in-Boots Game

Doctor Ligya was oh so right. I really loved the Puss-in-Boots game. I could have played every day. Most days, before the game, I'd visit with Maxwell and Blueberry in the parlor. We'd chew on our treats and stare at the huge painting of Sir Puss-in-Boots on the wall. The king of cats was magnificent to behold.

He was the most handsome cat we'd ever seen. His fur was glossy brown like a seal. He held his head high, making us proud we were from the CAT nation. His kingly smile was wonderful, showing his brilliantly white eye teeth. His striped tail was long like mine. He wore a vest and boots to his knees, a saber hung at his side. On his head he wore a huge chevalier's hat. He was glorious.

I felt like I was on an exciting roller coaster ride. I was now the number one Sir Puss-in-Boots game player in the Cat Hill Brain Training Academy. Puss was catching the mouse every time. I was excited. Human Mommy was excited. Human Papa was excited. Doctor Ligya was excited.

Doctor Ligya showed me and Human Mommy my brain waves. Strange looking things, moving up and down in a mountain of lines. I didn't understand what she was talking about. All I knew was my life had taken on a new meaning. I was a changed cat.

Today, I'm graduating with honors from the Cat Hill Brain Training Academy. Human Mommy dressed me up in a wide, bright yellow ribbon. She tied it in a big bow around my neck. My fur was brushed and shiny. I was almost out of my mind with happiness. I held my tail high. Still, all the attention made me nervous. Stop it, I told myself, relax. So I did.

Doctor Ligya was standing at the podium in the front of the fireplace. She was beautiful in her fancy black velvet dress, lace jacket and high heels. Human Mommy and Papa were also dressed to the nines. Amelia and Maxwell proudly stared at me, grinning. My other friends, Cashew, Foxie, Blueberry and Tiger smiled at me from the audience.

"Yoda, don't stand hidden in the back. Stand beside me here in front of your friends and family," Doctor Ligya said. "Ah...h. I hear a tapping on the window at the door. Come in, come in my dear friend and mentor. I was expecting you."

Puss-in-Boots Arrives for Yoda's Graduation

In walked Sir Puss-in-Boots, King of Cats, in all his kingly glory. He was almost as tall as Doctor Ligya. He went to the front of the parlor, smiling mischievously.

"I flew in from Paris this morning. I had received a call from Doctor Ligya regarding Yoda." He looked at his stunned audience. "I know many of you believe I am only a character in a French fairy tale. Not true. I'm a living being, King of the CAT NATION. I'm here today to present a special award to Yoda, cat daughter and lost princess of the kingdom of Xanadu. You can recognize the royal line by their extremely long tails.

My mouth dropped open. Human Mommy fainted in Human Papa's arms. He carried her to the couch and sat down himself. Amelia screamed. My cat friends mewed in unison and bowed their heads. I was so shocked I had to lean against Doctor Ligya.

"Yoda, my girl," Sir Puss strode to the front. "Come, sit on the chair Doctor Ligya prepared for you."

The walnut chair was ages old with a red velvet seat and back. I jumped onto the lamb fur pad, marking the place where I was to sit.

With his paw, Sir Puss picked up a golden graduation certificate and placed it next to me. My name appeared at the top with a list of my honors at the bottom. It was signed by Doctor Ligya, with a paw print from Sir Puss-in-Boots, King of the Cats. If I were human I think I would have fainted.

"Yoda," Sir Puss repeated, "is a daring, dauntless, darling cat whom I am proud to call sister. Her courageous desire to change her mind and her life began three months ago. This is the first time since the academy opened fifty years ago that such a reward has been given. Sister Princess, your mind is now as clear as crystal. You're ready to enter the world as the princess you are, bringing to your people your clear thinking and learning."

I turned my head shyly to look at the humans and cats who love me. Their eyes were glistening with pleasure. Human Mommy and Papa, Amelia and Doctor Ligya had tears in their eyes. If I were human, my eyes would have been full of tears too.

"Blessings on you dear sister," Sir Puss-in-Boots purred, "and may your life be filled with joy and happiness. I must go now. My work is never finished. I must return to Paris immediately. The CAT NATION'S Independence Day begins tomorrow. They expect me. Goodbye all.

We bowed our heads. When we looked up, he was gone.

Epilogue

"A letter's arrived for you, Doctor Ligya," Maxwell called, carrying the envelope in his mouth. He dropped it gently in front of her. "It's from Princess Yoda."

Doctor Ligya smiled. "Maxwell, join me. Come on up on my desk. Let's see what's happening in Yoda's life and how she's doing in the world with her new brain. I'll read it to you in CAT."

Dear human family, friends and cats,

I'm sorry I haven't written. I'm now going to Cat-lin High School. I'm at the top of my class. I've been so busy with my studies, I forget everything else. I feel badly. I've been neglectful. I sat down last night at my computer to write you all a very tardy thank you letter.

At the academy, I learned I don't need to run crazy. I can slow down and enjoy the roses, as humans say. I'm told I'm much more composed. No more the Chatty Catty that I was. I now enjoy my lounging time and can sleep quietly in the shade of my Human Mommy's holiday tree. I haven't broken one ornament, except by accident.

My wall running is over now and no more biting Easy's nose. I can tell he's relieved.

Oh yes, my focus is incredible. I play only one game at a time now. And, big wow, I'm beginning to understand human language. All it took was focus. Human Mommy and Papa are working hard to learn CAT, thanks to the book you sent them. This is true family happiness.

Sir Puss-in-Boots sends me an email once a week. He's looking forward to seeing me in Paris during summer vacation with my Human Mommy and Papa. He said he'd like me to talk with some of Paris' underground cats to encourage them with my story. I can't refuse him anything. I'm thinking I might go to the famous PRINCE of CATS UNIVERSITY in Paris when I graduate from high school. I've decided to study CAT history and teach it someday.

My life has changed so much. I admit though, I'm still not used to being called Princess Yoda. Oh well, life's a bliss so all is well. I thank Doctor Ligya and Sir Puss-in-Boots for believing in me. I thank my Human Mommy and Papa for loving me as I am. I thank Amelia for finding me. I also thank my war-torn buddy, Maxwell, for keeping me on the straight and narrow.

Love,

Princess Yoda

Notes of Interest

Yoda is a real life rescue cat. She lives with Doctor Victoria Ibric and her husband Doctor Andrew Peterson. They have a dog named Easy. Easy and Yoda are best animal friends. Yoda's story is true. She does have Attention Deficit/Hyperactivity Disorder (ADHD) and Reactive Attention Disorder (RAD).

In the early seventies, Doctor Barry Sterman, Ph.D., psycho-physiologist researcher, conducted Neurofeedback research studies at UCLA, using cats as his subjects. For the past fifty years, EEG Biofeedback or Neurofeedback have been used for various physical, emotional and mental conditions. Neurofeedback is also used for veterans with Post Traumatic Stress Disorder (PTSD) at various Neurofeedback centers and veteran medical facilities.

Doctor Victoria Ibric uses non-invasive Neurofeedback/EEG Biofeedback for brain training with children, teenagers, adults, and elders. Neurofeedback training is enhanced by the addition of the ROSHI system. The training program helps the brain to regulate by encouraging proper brain waves to occur which are related to the relaxation state and/or the focused state.

Over the years, Doctor Victoria Ibric and her colleagues found that the ROSHI system can be easily adapted for use with animals. The ROSHI system, was, in actuality, used on Yoda, Easy, and Tiger aka Maxwell to help them with their various symptoms. Another Neurofeedback therapist successfully used the ROSHI system on horses.

Puss in Boots is a French tale written by Charles Perrault, first published in 1697. Puss-in-Boots was left as an inheritance to the youngest son of a miller. He's no ordinary cat. Puss asks for and receives a pair of boots. Then he sets out on a magical quest to make his master's fortune. Puss has numerous adventures, ending with the Miller's son marrying a princess. Yoda's tale brings Puss-in-Boots to America to find the lost cat princess of Xanadu, opening a new chapter in his life. The final illustration includes the 19th century engraving of Puss in Boots, by Gustave Dore.

Cats do speak their own language. Their meows do mean something. When happy you may hear a cat mew, meow, murmur or purr. When a cat stalks a bird you may hear a chattering sound. When Mama Cat calls her kittens, you may hear a chirrup sound. When a cat is being aggressive, you may hear growls, yowls, snarls, hisses, spits, caterwauls or shrieks. Cats use various communication methods, and combinations thereof, to be understood within the cat community. Cats use a system of signs and symbols to convey information, i.e., hissing and arching their backs to ward off threats. Cats use all of their senses to communicate, such as vocal and sub-vocal sounds, facial and body language.

Note: most of the illustrations of Yoda show her as larger-then-life. This is a metaphor for how important she is in her family's life, how much they love her, and how proud they are of her.

Neurofeedback Information

Children, teenagers, and adults with Attention Deficit Disorder (ADD) or Attention Deficit /Hyperactivity Disorder (ADHD) respond specifically to the efficacy of Neurofeedback, helping to decrease or completely resolve the ADD/ADHD symptoms.

"Attention Deficit/Hyperactivity Disorder ADHS) has become one of the most common neurodevelopmental and psychiatric disorders of childhood...between 3% and 7% of school age children (Comier, 2008). In 40%-60% of all cases ADHD persists into adolescence and adulthood (Faraone, Biederman, & Mick, 2006)." The core symptoms of ADHD consist of inattention, impulsivity, and hyperactivity.

"Neurofeedback has met the highest standards currently being applied to the appraisal of psychosocial interventions." Neurofeedback has been evaluated for more than fifty years and is practiced worldwide. Neurofeedback has been proven to be at Efficacy Level 5...statistically efficacious and specific for ADD/ADHD.

"Due to the inclusion of some very recent and sound methodological studies...the clinical effects of Neurofeedback in the treatment of ADHD can be regarded as clinically meaningful."

At the Neurofeedback & NeuroRehab Institute, Inc., we use non-invasive Neurofeedback instruments in conjunction with the ROSHI System. The institute administers brain mapping (QEEG, quantitative EEG), conducts psychological and neurological assessments, and a nutritional analysis. Periodically, an evaluation of a client's brain training progress is obtained. The results are discussed with the client. We strive to retrain the brain to function at its peak level of performance.

ADD/ADHD Evaluation

Please rate yourself, or the person you're evaluating, on each of the symptoms listed below using the following scale. If possible, as a second opinion, have another family member rate you or the other individual. This is done to obtain a more complete picture of the condition.

0 – Never   1 – Rarely   2 – Occasionally
3 – Frequently   4 – Very Frequently
NA – Not Applicable

Self	Others	Symptoms
		1. is easily distracted
		2. has difficulty sustaining attention span for most tasks in play, school, or work
		3. has trouble listening when others are talking
		4. has difficulty follow through (procrastinating) on tasks or instructions
		5. has difficulty keeping an organized area (room, desk, book bag, locker, etc
		6. has trouble with time, i.e., frequently late or hurried, tasks taking longer than expected, projects/homework completed last minute or turned in late
		7. has tendency to lose things

		8. forgetful
		9. makes careless mistakes, poor attention to detail
		10. daydreams excessively
		11. complains of being bored
		12. appears apathetic or unmotivated
		13. is tired, sluggish, or slow moving
		14. is spacey or seems preoccupied
		15. is restless or hyperactive
		16. has trouble sitting still
		17. is fidgety, in constant motion (hands, feet, body)
		18. noisy, has a hard time being quiet
		19. acts as if driven by a motor
		20. talks excessively
		21. impulsive, doesn't think through comments or actions before they're said or done
		22. has difficulty waiting his or her turn
		23. interrupts or intrudes, i.e., butts into conversations or games

References

www.Neurofeedback-dribric.com

www.amenclinic.com

www.skiltopo.com

http://www.eegfeedback.org/joelbio.html

"ADD: The Twenty-Hour Solution, Attention Deficit Disorder and the Healing Effects," by Mark Steinberg Ph.D. and Sigfried Othmer, Ph.D.

Moss, D. & Gunkelman, J. (2002). Task force report on methodology and empirically support treatments: introduction and summary, *Biofeedback*, 30 (2), 19-20. www.aapb.org and www.snr-jnt.org.

Beauregard & Levesque, (2006); Levesque, Beauregard & Mensour, (2006).

American Academy of Pediatrics Recognizes Neurofeedback for ADHD (Oct.2012). AAP gave Neurofcedback their top rating in application to the behavioral symptoms of ADHD.

Brainclinics Diagnostics (M.Arns), Brainclinics Treatment (S. de Ridder), EEG Resource Institute (M.Breteler), Radboud University (M.Breteler, A. Coenen), Nijrnegen, The Netherlands; and the University of Tuebingen (U. Strehl), Germany. "Efficacy of Neurofeed-back Treatment in ADHD; the Effects on Inattention, Impulsivity and Hyperactivity: a Meta-Analysis." *Clinical EEG and Neuroscience* (2009), vol. 40, no.3, 180.

Arns, M., et al. Evaluation of Neurofeedback in ADHD: The long and winding road. *Biol. Psychol.* (2013). http://dx.doi.org10,1016/ j.biopscho. 2013.11.013

www.fairytales.co/puss_in_boots.html

messybeast.com/cat_talk2.htm

en.wikipedia.org/wiki/Cat

About the Author

A lover of books, Joan A. de Bruin has made up stories since she was a child. Blending writing and art, she uses duality, metaphor, common sayings, fables and fairy tales to enrich her children and adult fiction.

She is at work on an adult suspense novel, *Life/Line*, and a family story, *The Christmas Tree Angel*, both set in Los Angeles. And, working on a new paint series, *Eyes in the Universe*.

Joan A. de Bruin is the former Director of the L.A. Craft & Folk Art Museum, Founder of artbridgegallery.com, fiction writer, studio artist, and art educator.

Joan A. de Bruin